THE IMITATION OF BUDDHA

THE IMITATION OF BUDDHA

Quotations from Buddhist Literature for each Day in the Year.

COMPILED BY

ERNEST M. BOWDEN

WITH PREFACE BY

SIR EDWIN ARNOLD, K.C.I.E., C.S.I.

The Buddha has mercy even on the meanest thing,
Cullavagga.

GYAN

Published by

Gyan Publishing House
5, Ansari Road
Daryaganj, New Delhi-110002
Phone: 011-47034999, 9811692060
E-mail: books@gyanbooks.com

Distribution Network
gyanbooks.com
India, USA, Canada, UK, Australia, France

ISBN : 978-81-212-2400-0 (PB)
First Published, 1893

2nd Impression 2021

Printed at: Gyan Press, Delhi.

The
Imitation of Buddha
Compiled by: Ernest M. Bowden

THE

IMITATION OF BUDDHA

Quotations from Buddhist Literature for each Day in the Year.

COMPILED BY

ERNEST M. BOWDEN

WITH PREFACE BY

SIR EDWIN ARNOLD, K.C.I.E., C.S.I.

The Buddha has mercy even on the meanest thing.
Cullavagga.

Methuen & Co.,

18, BURY STREET, LONDON, W.C.

1893.

PREFACE.

I AM glad to be permitted thus to say, in a few words of introduction to this well-meditated little volume, how pleasant and how profitable an idea it must be considered to have designed and compiled a Buddhist anthology. Selecting his cut and uncut jewels from very various Buddhistic sources, Mr. Bowden has here supplied those who buy and use the book with rubies and sapphires and emeralds of wisdom, compassion and human brotherhood, any one of which, worn on the heart, would be sufficient to make the wearer rich beyond estimation for a day. The author disclaims any attempt to set forth a *corpus* of Buddhistic morality and doctrine, nor, indeed, would anything of the kind be possible within such narrow limits; but I rejoice to observe how well and faithfully his manifold extracts from the Sacred books of India and the East exhibit that ever-pervading tenderness of the great Asiatic Teacher, which extended itself to all alike that live. This compassionateness of Gautama, if nothing else had been illustrated by the collection, would render it precious to possess and fruitful to employ; but many another lofty tenet of the "Light" of Asia finds illumination in some brief verse or maxim, as day after day glides by; and he who should mark the passage of the months from January to December with these simple pages must become, I think, a better man at the year's end than at its beginning. I recommend the "Imitation of Buddha" without hesitation or reserve.

EDWIN ARNOLD.

London, March 31*st*, 1891.

COMPILER'S PROEM.

In this modest compilation, no attempt has been made to present a general view of Buddhism as a religious or philosophical system. The aim has been, not so much to expound Buddhism, or any one phase or development of it, as to utilise Buddhism to teach the highest morality; and this with some special reference to that praiseworthy feature in the Buddhist code—its inclusion of every sentient creature within the sphere of our duties and sympathies.

In respect of our duty to the lower animals, we may look upon Buddhist morality as rather supplementary to Christian, or at all events to Christian morality as apparently understood, for instance, in such a representative work as the famous "Imitation of Christ." It must not, however, be thought that the design and the title of the "Imitation of Buddha" evince any cynical or hostile spirit towards the religion of Christendom. Whatever one's personal predilections, nothing could be more unseemly, or less in keeping with the nature one attributes to the Buddha, than wantonly to set up two such characters as Buddha and Christ in a sort of hostile rivalry for our esteem and imitation. At the same time one cannot but remark on the entire absence from so many Christian treatises of all sympathetic or moral allusion to the lower orders of life, an absence the more unfortunate when a reasoned attempt has even been made, on the strength of Christian teaching, to explode the notion that we owe duties to animals, (*e.g.* in "Moral

Philosophy," by Father Joseph Rickaby). Very different on this point is the tone of the average Buddhist treatise, with its formal exhortations, recurring as a matter of course, to show mercy upon every living thing; and this difference it is which is mainly responsible for the appearance of the present volume.

The sacred and semi-sacred compositions of the Buddhists contain plenty of inconsistencies, much that is tame and pointless, and some things even repulsive. But from this voluminous literature, or rather from those parts of it rendered into English or French from some eight or ten Eastern languages, a selection has been made of the noble precepts and beautiful sentiments, which are scattered at random through Buddhist works. We need not here inquire too closely how much of so-called Buddhism is probably due to the gentle and high-souled Buddha himself: enough that these lofty ideals of righteous conduct, these earnest presentments of the noble and the good, have all gathered around the name and the system of Buddha.

While some of the passages quoted might gain, some on the other hand would undoubtedly lose, if taken in connection with other words in the original which occur in close proximity. No pretence, however, is made of bringing out the weak points in Buddhism; nor is anything further attempted than to avoid wilfully perverting the meaning of any passage or phrase by isolation from its context.

In regard to the sources quoted from, considerable latitude seemed allowable. They do not all by any means possess canonical authority. But all of them, if not canonical, are either distinctly Buddhist in character, or else, in the part quoted from, are treating of Buddhism. The supposed dates of the originals range from at least the third century B.C. to mediæval or even later times.

It will thus be clear that should anyone think to make use of quotations in the "Imitation of Buddha" for controversial purposes, a certain degree of caution will be necessary. For one thing, the religious terms—for example, 'heaven' and 'sin'—which have to be employed in English translations, do not always correspond exactly to the Buddhist notion. For another thing, the translators themselves are not always at one as to the sense of the originals. And besides this, for some purposes at all events, not only the context of the passage, but the date, the authorship, and the whole character of the original work might have to be taken into account. Those who have ready access to such information are hardly likely to need any help which the present compilation could afford.

The insertion of a passage in this Buddhist anthology does not of necessity indicate that the belief implied in the passage is accepted; nor is it quite meant that the moral maxims should in every instance be acted upon literally. Concerning that oft-repeated injunction not to kill any living creature whatsoever, we can hardly doubt that there are many cases in which to take away life, provided it be taken painlessly, not only is not on the whole an unkindness, but is an act of beneficence. If we sometimes give to this injunction the sense rather of extending our sympathy to the lowliest sentient being, and not causing pain to living creatures *while* they live, we shall, perhaps, not be doing violence to the spirit of mercy by which the injunction was prompted. In this connection, with all possible reverence for the earnestness of Buddha, and with every wish not to set up in his name a travesty of his teaching, we may note the several passages in Buddhist works which inculcate preference for the spirit over the letter, or the exercise of judgment in accepting what we are taught. Here is one: "Be sure that you tell me the spirit [of the doctrine]; I want but the spirit; why do you make so much of the letter?" (Mahâvagga, khandhaka 1, chap. 23, sec. 4.) And again, though from a less authoritative source: "The learned must examine my commandments and receive them accordingly, and not out of respect [for me]." (Quoted in Csoma's "Grammar of the Tibetan Language.")

To the injunctions which seem to countenance indiscriminate alms-giving, we may no doubt impart with advantage the sense of doing beneficent work of some kind or other with our wealth.

No individual translator must be held responsible for the exact form of expression adopted in the passages quoted. In some instances, two translations of the same composition have been compared. But even where this is not so, it has frequently been impossible, without, not only uncouthness, but obscurity, to retain in these brief, isolated quotations from Buddhist sources, precisely the translator's language. Partly for this reason, the references given are to the originals, not to the English translations; and therefore a general indication of the channels through which the substance of the passages was obtained, may not be undesirable here. The following translations and other works include most of those which have proved directly helpful for the purpose in hand:—

"Sacred Books of the East," namely:—

Vol. 10. "Dhammapada," by F. Max Müller; and "Sutta-Nipâta," by V. Fausböll.

Vol. 11. "Buddhist Suttas," by T. W. Rhys Davids.

Vol. 13. "Vinaya Texts," part 1, by T. W. Rhys Davids & H. Oldenberg.

Vol. 17. "Vinaya Texts," part 2, by T. W. Rhys Davids & H. Oldenberg

Vol. 19. "Fo-sho-hing-tsan-king," by Rev. S. Beal.

Vol. 20. "Vinaya Texts," part 3, by T. W. Rhys Davids & H. Oldenberg.

Vol. 21. "Saddharma-pu*nd*arîka," by H. Kern.

Vol. 35. "Questions of King Milinda," part 1, by T. W. Rhys Davids.

Vol. 36. "Questions of King Milinda," part 2, by T. W. Rhys Davids.

"Travels of Fâ-hien," by James Legge.

"Selected Essays," by F. Max Müller.

"Buddhist Birth Stories, or Jātaka Tales," by T. W. Rhys Davids.

"Hibbert Lectures for 1881," by T. W. Rhys Davids.

"Buddhism," by T. W. Rhys Davids.

"Catena of Buddhist Scriptures from the Chinese," by Rev. S. Beal.

"Abstract of Four Lectures on Buddhist Literature in China," by Rev. S. Beal.

"Romantic Legend of Sâkya Buddha," by Rev. S. Beal.

"Texts from the Buddhist Canon known as Dhammapada," by Rev. S. Beal.

"Udânavarga," by W. W. Rockhill.

"Lalita Vistara," by Rájendralála Mitra.

"Sanskrit Buddhist Literature of Nepal," by Rájendralála Mitra.

"Mahávaṇsa," by L. C. Wijesinha.

"Attanagalu-vansa," by James D'Alwis.

"Archæological Survey of Southern India," (new series of reports), vol. 1, by James Burgess, with translations by Georg Bühler.

"Archæological Survey of Western India," vol. 4, by James Burgess.

"Sutta - Nipáta," by Sir M. Coomára Swámy.

"Kathá Sarit Ságara," by C. H. Tawney.

"Grammar of the Tibetan Language," by A. Csoma de Kőrös.

"Nágánanda: a Buddhist Drama," by Palmer Boyd.

"Buddhaghosha's Parables," by Capt. T. Rogers.

"Light of Asia," by Sir Edwin Arnold.

"Ancient Proverbs and Maxims from Burmese Sources," by James Gray.

"The English Governess at the Siamese Court," by Mrs. A. H. Leonowens.

"The Catechism of the Shamans," by C. F. Neumann.

"View of the History, Literature, and Religion of the Hindoos," by Rev. W. Ward.

"Horæ Sinicæ: Translations from the Popular Literature of the Chinese," by Rev. Robert Morrison.

Contemporary Review for February, 1876.

Cornhill Magazine for August, 1876.

The Buddhist, vol. 1.

Journal of Pâli Text Society for 1886.

Journal of Royal Asiatic Society, new series, vol. 2.

Journal of Ceylon Branch of Royal Asiatic Society, no. 2.

Journal of Asiatic Society of Bengal, vol. 36.

Journal of American Oriental Society, vol. 4.

Journal Asiatique, septième série, vols. 17, 19, and 20.

"Lalita Vistara," by P. É. Foucaux.

"La Guirlande Précieuse des Demandes et des Réponses," by P. É. Foucaux.

"Sept Suttas Pâlis, tirés du Dîgha-nikâya," by P. Grimblot.

With a few unimportant exceptions, the quotations in this book have all been made with the kind permission of either the authors or the publishers of the translations used: for granting which permissions, cordial thanks are due, among others, to Professor Max Müller, Sir Edwin Arnold, and Mr. Rhys Davids. The compiler would express, in a special degree, his indebtedness to the volumes above mentioned of the "Sacred Books of the East," published by the Clarendon Press, which have probably yielded fully half the passages quoted. Cordial thanks also are due for the permission to quote granted by Messrs. Kegan Paul, Trench, Trübner, and Co., by whom a large proportion of the above works are issued.

E. M. B.

January.

1.

ALL beings desire happiness; therefore to all extend your benevolence.

Mahâvaṁsa (ch. 12).

2.

BECAUSE he has pity upon every living creature, therefore is a man called 'holy.'*

Dhammapada (v. 270).

3.

LIKE as a mother at the risk of her life watches over her ... only child, so also let every one cultivate towards all beings a boundless (friendly) mind.

Metta-sutta (v. 7).

* Ariya.

4.

Hurt not others with that which pains yourself.

Udânavarga (ch. 5, v. 18).

5.

Identifying himself with others.

Nâlaka-sutta (v. 27).

The king is to us even as a father; he loves us even as he loves himself; we are to the king even as (his) children.

Rock Inscriptions of Asoka
(Separate edicts, no. 2).

6.

With pure thoughts and fulness of love, I will do towards others what I do for myself.

Lalita Vistara (ch. 5).

7.

He lives only to be a help to others.

Questions of King Milinda (Book 4, ch. 2, sec. 30).

8.

Why should we cling to this perishable body? In the eye of the wise, the only thing it is good for is to benefit one's fellow-creatures.

Kathâ Sarit Sâgara (ch. 28).

9.

Is not all I possess, even to my very body, kept for the benefit of others?

Nâgânanda (act 1).

10.

FORBEARANCE was our Buddha wont to teach.

Mahâparinibbâna-sutta (ch. 6).

11.

THOUGH a man with a sharp sword should cut one's body bit by bit, let not an angry thought ... arise, let the mouth speak no ill word.

Fo-sho-hing-tsan-king (v. 2,046).

12.

THEM who became thy murderers, thou forgavest.

Lalita Vistara (ch. 13).

13.

Overcome evil by good.

Udânavarga (ch. 20, v. 18).

14.

Conquer your foe by force, and you increase his enmity; conquer by love, and you reap no after-sorrow.

Fo-sho-hing-tsan-king (v. 2,241).

15.

This great principle of returning good for evil.

Sûtra of Forty-two Sections (sec. 7).

16.

The member of Buddha's order...should not intentionally destroy the life of any being, down even to a worm or an ant.

Mahâvagga (khandhaka 1, ch. 78).

17.

Whether now any man kill with his own hand, or command any other to kill, or whether he only see with pleasure the act of killing—all is equally forbidden by this law, and many other things which cannot be described one by one.

Sha-mi-lu-i-yao-lio.

18.

My teaching is this, that the slightest act of charity, even in the lowest class of persons, such as saving the life of an insect out of pity, that this act ... shall bring to the doer of it consequent benefit.

T'sa-ho-hom-king (sutta 2).

19.

He came to remove the sorrows of all living things.

Fo-sho-hing-tsan-king (v. 35).

He who holds up a torch to (lighten) mankind is always honoured by me.

Râhula-sutta (v. 2).

20.

Aims so high, and endeavours so grand.

Questions of King Milinda
(Book 4, ch. 1, sec. 41).

21.

"Now (said he) I will seek a noble law, unlike the worldly methods known to men, ... and will fight against the mischief wrought upon man by sickness, age, and death."

Fo-sho-hing-tsan-king (v. 339).

22.

THE prince has grown up in a palace, with every care bestowed upon his tender person; and now he gives his body to the ... thorny forest: how shall he bear a life of privation?

Fo-sho-hing-tsan-king (vv. 446-7).

23.

THAT you who of right might rule the earth, ... should now go begging here and there your food! ... not receiving the tribute of the world, but begging food sufficient for ... nourishment!

Fo-sho-hing-tsan-king (vv. 1548-50).

24.

THOU flower of all thy race! confessedly the most renowned! ... ever reverenced without self-seeking! ... thou who wert wont to repose upon a soft and kingly couch! ... how canst thou endure the mountain and the forest wilds, on the bare grass to make thyself a resting-place?

Fo-sho-hing-tsan-king (vv. 604-6).

25.

All men should cultivate a fixed and firm determination, and vow that what they once undertake they will never give up.

Fo-pen-hing-tsih-king (ch. 31).

26.

May my body be ground to powder small as the mustard-seed if I ever desire to (break my vow)!

Fo-pen-hing-tsih-king (ch. 25).

27.

This, though I gained heaven's high state, cannot be done! How much less to gain an earthly ... home!

Fo-sho-hing-tsan-king (v. 726).

Rather will I fall headlong into this hell, ... than do a deed that is unworthy.

Jâtaka 40.

28.

HAPPY is he that is virtuous.

Dhammapada (v. 18).

To make an end of selfishness is happiness.

Udânavarga (ch. 30, v. 26).

29.

THERE is no happiness except in righteousness.

Attanagalu-vansa (ch. 2, sec. 14).

30.

FULL of love for all things in the world, practising virtue in order to benefit others—this man only is happy.

Fa-kheu-pi-ü (sec. 39).

31.

He that loveth iniquity, beckoneth to misfortune.

Jitsu-go-kiyô.

February.

1.

WATCH your thoughts.

Dhammapada (v. 327).

CONTROL your tongue.

Dhammapada (v. 232).

2.

BE pure and live with the pure.

Dhammacariya-sutta (v. 10).

PURE in word and deed and heart.

Questions of King Milinda
(Book 4, ch. 4, sec. 43).

3.

THE higher life maketh he known, in all its purity and in all its perfectness.

Tevijja-sutta (ch. 1).

4.

To save countless beings,
Not omitting even the least in his intention.

Phû-yau-king (kiouen 2).

5.

THE birds and beasts and creeping things—
'tis writ—
Had sense of Buddha's vast embracing love,
And took the promise of his piteous speech.

Sir Edwin Arnold (*Light of Asia*, bk. 8).

6.

ON first awaking from my sleep,
I should pray that every breathing thing
May wake to saving wisdom, vast
As the wide and boundless universe.

Daily Manual of the Shaman.

7.

He cherished the feeling of affection for all beings as if they were his only son.

Lalita Vistara (ch. 13).

8.

Closely as cause and effect are bound together,
So do two loving hearts entwine and live—
Such is the power of love to join in one.

Fo-pen-hing-tsih-king (ch. 47).

9.

Full of compassion for every living being.

Saddharma-puṇḍarîka (ch. 3, v. 143).

That thou mayst know—
What others will not—that I loved thee most
Because I loved so well all living souls.

Sir Edwin Arnold (*Light of Asia*, bk. 4).

10.

There is no sweet companion like pure charity.

Fo-sho-hing-tsan-king (v. 1,508).

11.

Ever exercising love towards the infirm.

Fa-kheu-pi-ü (sec. 7).

Exceedingly loving towards the people, and whose hearts melt with pity.

Ajanta Cave Inscriptions.

12.

Ever inspired by pity and love to men.

Fo-sho-hing-tsan-king (v. 460).

13.

Good is restraint in all things.

Dhammapada (v. 361).

Unselfish, true, and self-controlled.

Jâtaka 31.

14.

The religious mendicant, wisely reflecting, is patient under cold and heat, under hunger and thirst, ... under bodily suffering, under pains however sharp.

Sabbâsava-sutta (sec. 29).

15.

Though a man conquer a thousand thousand men in battle, a greater conqueror still is he who conquers himself.

Udânavarga (ch. 23, v. 3).

16.

ROOT out the love of self.

Jâtaka 25.

17.

THE man of honour should minister to his friends ... by liberality, courtesy, benevolence, and by doing to them as he would be done by.

Sigâlovâda-sutta.

18.

PRACTISE the art of 'giving up.'*

Fo-sho-hing-tsan-king (v. 1,442).

* *I.e.*, putting away all desire and giving up 'self.'

19.

SPEAK not harshly to anybody.

Dhammapada (v. 133).

20.

MAY I speak kindly and softly to everyone I chance to meet.

Inscription in Temple of Nakhon Vat.

21.

LET him not, even though irritated, speak harsh words.

Sâriputta-sutta (v. 17).

OFFENSIVE language is harsh even to the brutes.

Suttavaḍḍhananîti (v. 16).

22.

WHATEVER word is humane ... and lovely, reaching to the heart, ... pleasing to the people, beloved of the people—such are the words he speaks.

Tevijja-sutta (ch. 2).

23.

LET him neither be led into falsehood, nor consciously do wicked things.

Tuvaṭaka-sutta (v. 17).

24.

LET a man say that which is right, not that which is unrighteous, ... that which is pleasing, not that which is unpleasing, ... that which is true, not that which is false.

Subhâsita-sutta (v. 1).

25.

As he who loves life avoids poison, so let the sage avoid sinfulness.

Udánavarga (ch. 28, v. 14).

26.

He sees danger in even the least of those things he should avoid.

Tevijja-sutta (ch. 1).

Sin easily develops.

Rock Inscriptions of Asoka (edict 5).

27.

May I never do, nor cause to be done, nor contemplate the doing of, even the most trivial sin!

Attanagalu-vansa (conclusion.)

28.

To be firm and resolute as iron.

Ta-chwang-yan-king-lun (sermon 62).

A FIRM but loving heart.

Ta-chwang-yan-king-lun (sermon 62).

29.

LET not one who is asked for his pardon withhold it.

Mahâvagga (khandhaka 1, ch. 27).

'TIS wrong to conquer him who sues for mercy.

Lalita Vistara (ch. 3).

March.

1.

Let none out of anger or resentment wish harm to another.

Metta-sutta (v. 6).

2.

Let us then live happily, not hating those who hate us. In the midst of those who hate us, let us dwell free from hatred.

Dhammapada (v. 197).

3.

For hatred does not cease by hatred at any time; hatred ceases by love; this is an old rule.

Dhammapada (v. 5).

4.

(To the) self-reliant there is strength and joy.

Fo-sho-hing-tsan-king (v. 1,777).

5.

LET him not grieve for that which is lost.

Attadaṇḍa-sutta (v. 10).

NOT from weeping or grieving will any obtain peace of mind.

Salla-sutta (v. 11).

6.

AT first my sorrowing heart was heavy; but now my sorrow has brought forth only profit.

Fo-sho-hing-tsan-king (v. 1,572).

7.

Give to him that asketh, even though it be but a little.

Udânavarga (ch. 20, v. 15).

8.

Your guileless heart loves to exercise its charity.

Fo-sho-hing-tsan-king (v. 1,502).

Those in whom there is neither deceit nor arrogance, who are free from cupidity, selfishness, desire, upon such in due time should people bestow their offerings.

Mâgha-sutta (v. 8).

9.

He delights in giving so far as he is able.

Questions of King Milinda
Book 4, ch. 1, sec. 9).

10.

Earnestly practise every good work.

Fo-sho-hing-tsan-king (v. 1,981).

11.

Not to be weary in well-doing.

Mahâmangala-sutta (v. 7).

A hero in beneficence.

Lalita Vistara (ch. 13).

12.

Pure in morals, and assiduous in doing good.

Saddharma-puṇḍarika (ch. 8, v. 24).

13.

MAKE no idols of any kind.

Siamese Buddhist Maxim.

WHEN pure rules of conduct are observed, then there is true religion.

Fo-sho-hing-tsan-king (v. 2,027).

14.

WHEREIN does religion consist?

In (committing) the least possible harm, in (doing) abundance of good, in (the practice of) pity, love, truth, and likewise purity of life.

Pillar Inscriptions of Asoka (edict 2).

15.

(NOT superstitious rites, but) kindness to slaves and servants, reverence towards venerable persons, self-control with respect to living creatures, ... these and similar (virtuous actions are the rites which ought indeed to be performed).

Rock Inscriptions of Asoka (edict 9).

16.

THE practice of religion involves as a first principle a loving, compassionate heart for all creatures.

Fo-pen-hing-tsih-king (ch. 21).

17.

SHALL we in worshipping slay that which hath life? This is like those who practise wisdom, and the way of religious abstraction, but neglect the rules of moral conduct.

Fo-sho-hing-tsan-king (v. 905).

18.

How can a system requiring the infliction of misery on other beings be called a religious system? ... To seek a good by doing an evil is surely no safe plan.

Fo-pen-hing-tsih-king (ch. 20).

19.

Unto the dumb lips of his flock he lent
Sad pleading words, showing how man, who prays
For mercy to the gods, is merciless.

Sir Edwin Arnold (*Light of Asia*, bk. 5).

20.

I then will ask you, If a man, in worshipping, ... sacrifices a sheep, and so does well, wherefore not his child, ... and so do better? Surely ... there is no merit in killing a sheep!

Fo-pen-king-tsih-king (ch. 20).

21.

Nor [shall one] lay
Upon the brow of innocent bound beasts
One hair's weight of that answer all must give
For all things done amiss or wrongfully.

Sir Edwin Arnold (*Light of Asia*, bk. 5).

22.

DOING no injury to anyone,
Dwell in the world full of love and kindness.

Questions of King Milinda
(Book 4, ch. 3, sec. 35).

23.

MINISTERING to the worthy, doing harm to none,
Always ready to render reverence to whom it is due,
Loving righteousness and righteous conversation,
Ever willing to hear what may profit another.

Fo-pen-hing-tsih-king (ch. 38).

24.

SCRUPULOUSLY avoiding all wicked actions
Reverently performing all virtuous ones;
Purifying his intention from all selfish ends:
This is the doctrine of all the Buddhas.

Siau-chi-kwan.

25.

INSTRUCT yourself (more and more) in the highest morality.

Nâgârjuna's 'Friendly Epistle' (v. 53).

26.

THEY must cultivate a feeling of deep shame for their sin.

Siau-chi-kwan (sec. 1).

27.

MAY my thoughts, now small and narrow, expand in the next existence, that I may understand the precepts ... thoroughly, and never break them or be guilty of trespasses.

Inscription in Temple of Nakhon Vat.

28.

Religion he looks upon as his best ornament.

Fo-sho-hing-tsan-king (v. 1,774).

The sinner is never beautiful.

Lalita Vistara (ch. 12).

29.

Use no perfume but sweetness of thoughts.

Siamese Buddhist Maxim.

30.

Wealth and beauty, scented flowers and ornaments like these, are not to be compared for grace with moral rectitude!

Fo-sho-hing-tsan-king (v. 1,790).

31.

Beautiful is she beyond conception, having the beauty of the noblest of womankind.

Lalita Vistara (ch. 3).

Look not upon a woman unchastely.

Siamese Buddhist Maxim.

April.

I.

Ask not of (a person's) descent, but ask about his conduct.

Sundarikabhâradvâja-sutta (v. 9).

2.

The young man Vâseṭṭha said: "When one is virtuous and full of (good) works, in this way he becomes a Brâhmaṇa."

Vâseṭṭha-sutta (preamble).

3.

Not by birth does one become low caste, not by birth a Brâhmaṇa; by his deeds he becomes low caste, by his deeds he becomes a Brâhmaṇa.

Vasala-sutta (v. 21).

4.

THAT man who ... speaks falsely when asked as a witness, let us know such as a 'base-born.'

Vasala-sutta (v. 7).

5.

WHOSOEVER takes dishonestly the property of others, ... or (repudiates his lawful debts), let us know such as a 'base-born.'

Vasala-sutta (vv. 4-5).

6.

WHOSOEVER ... harms living beings, ... and in whom there is no compassion for them, let us know such as a 'base-born.'

Vasala-sutta (v. 2).

7.

In whom there is truth and righteousness, he is blessed, he is a Brâhmaṇa.

Dhammapada (v. 393).

8.

Whoso hurts not (living) creatures, whether those that tremble or those that are strong, nor yet kills nor causes to be killed, him do I call a Brâhmaṇa.

Vâseṭṭha-sutta (v. 36).

9.

Whoso is (entirely) divested of sin, as is the heaven of mire and the moon of dust. him do I call a Brâhmaṇa.

Udânavarga (ch. 33, v. 38).

10.

Him I call indeed a Brâhmaṇa who, though he be guilty of no offence, patiently endures reproaches, bonds, and stripes.

Dhammapada (v. 399).*

11.

We will ... patiently suffer ... threats and blows ... at the hands of foolish men.

Saddharma-puṇḍarîka (ch. 12, v. 3).

Who, though he be cursed by the world, yet cherishes no ill-will towards it.

Sammâparibbâjaniya-sutta (v. 8).

12.

Persecutions and revilings, murders and numberless imprisonments, these hast thou suffered in thousands from the world, verily delighting in long-suffering.

Lalita Vistara (ch. 13).

* See also Vâseṭṭha-sutta (v. 30), and Udâna varga (ch. 33, v. 20).

13.

At the end of life the soul goes forth alone; whereupon only our good deeds befriend us.

Fo-sho-hing-tsan-king (v. 1,560).

14.

The wrongdoer, devoid of rectitude, ... is full of anxiety when death arrives.

Mahâparinibbâna-sutta (ch. 1).

He who has done what is right is free from fear.

Udânavarga (ch. 28, v. 31).

15.

Whatsoever a man has done, whether virtuous or sinful deeds, not one of them is of little importance; they all bear some kind of fruit.

Udânavarga (ch. 9, v. 8).

16.

OUR deeds, whether good or evil, ... follow us as shadows.

Fo-sho-hing-tsan-king (v. 1,629).

17.

HE who now gives in charity
Shall surely reap where he has given;
For whosoever piously bestows a little water,
Shall receive return like the great ocean.

Ta-chwang-yan-king-lun (sermon 20).

18.

COVETOUS desire is the greatest (source of) sorrow. Appearing as a friend, in secret 'tis our enemy.

Fo-sho-hing-tsan-king (v. 1,813).

19.

THAT which is given in charity is rich in returns; therefore charity is a true friend; although it scatters it brings no remorse.

Fo-sho-hing-tsan-king (v. 833).

20.

HE who ... stints the profit he has made, his wealth will soon be spent and lost.

Fo-sho-hing-tsan-king (v. 832).

21.

THE (real) treasure is that laid up ... through charity and piety, temperance and self-control. ... The treasure thus hid is secure, and passes not away. Though he leave the fleeting riches of the world, this a man carries with him—a treasure that no wrong of others, and no thief, can steal.

Nidhikaṇḍa-sutta.

22.

THOUGH exalted, forget not the lowly.

Jitsu-go-kiyô.

23.

BE kind to all that lives.

Fo-sho-hing-tsan-king (v. 2,024).

NOT hurting any creature.

Khaggavisâṇa-sutta (v. 1).

24.

EXALTED by his virtues, but lowly through modesty

Ajanta Cave Inscriptions.

25.

Of all possessions, contentedness is the best by far.

Nâgârjuna's 'Friendly Epistle' (v. 34).

A contented mind is always joyful.

Fo-sho-hing-tsan-king (v. 2,060).

26.

Let us then live happily, though we call nothing our own.

Dhammapada (v. 200).

27.

Not the whole world, ... the ocean-girt earth,
With all the seas and the hills that girdle it,
Would I wish to possess with shame added thereto.

Questions of King Milinda
(Book 4, ch. 5, sec. 17).

28.

Let none be forgetful of his own duty for the sake of another's.

Dhammapada (v. 166).

29.

The faults of others are easily seen: ... one's own faults are difficult to see.

Udânavarga (ch. 27, v. 1).

Self-examination is painful.

Pillar Inscriptions of Asoka (edict 3).

30.

A man winnows his neighbour's faults like chaff: his own he hides, as a cheat the bad die from the gambler.

Dhammapada (v. 252).

May.

I.

SHE orders her household aright, she is hospitable to kinsmen and friends, a chaste wife, a thrifty housekeeper, skilful and diligent in all her duties.

Sigâlovâda-sutta.

2.

LET him not cause others to drink, nor even approve of those that drink.

Dhammika-sutta (v. 23).

A GAMBLER is not fit to support a wife.

Sigâlovâda-sutta.

3.

THE wife ... should be cherished by her husband. *Sigâlovâda-sutta.*

CARING for father and mother, ... properly fostering wife and child, ... taking thought for his friends, ... patiently continuing in the way of duty. *Fa-kheu-pi-ü* (sec. 39).

4.

IT is better to die in righteousness than to live in unrighteousness.

Loweda Sangrahaya.

5.

BETTER to fling away life than transgress our convictions of duty.

Ta-chwang-yan-king-lun (sermon 44).

6.

BETTER for me to die battling (with the tempter), than that I should live defeated.

Padhâna-sutta (v. 16).

7.

The loving Father * of all that lives.

Tsing-tu-wan.

Our loving Father, and Father of all that breathes.—*Daily Manual of the Shaman.*

8.

Even so of all things that have ... life, there is not one that (the Buddhist anchorite) passes over; ... he looks upon all with ... deep-felt love. This, verily, ... is the way to a state of union with God.†

Tevijja-sutta (ch. 3).

9.

Doubts will exist as long as we live in the
world.
Yet, pursuing with joy the road of virtue,
Like the man who observes the rugged
path along the precipice, we ought
Gladly and profitably to follow it.

Siau-chi-kwan (sec. 3).

* *I.e.*, Amitâbha. † Brahmâ.

10.

To feed a single good man is infinitely greater in point of merit, than attending to questions about heaven and earth, spirits and demons, such as occupy ordinary men.

Sûtra of Forty-two Sections (sec. 10).

11.

CULTIVATING a pitiful and loving heart.

Ta-chwang-yan-king-lun (sermon 62).

WHAT is goodness? First and foremost the agreement of the will with the conscience.

Sûtra of Forty-two Sections (sec. 13).

12.

IF you remove (from conduct) the purpose of the mind, the bodily act is but as rotten wood. Wherefore regulate the mind, and the body of itself will go right.

Fo-sho-hing-tsan-king (v. 527).

13.

KEEP watch over your hearts.

Mahâparinibbâna-sutta (ch. 3).

LET no evil desire whatever arise within you. *Cullavagga* (khandhaka 7, ch. 4).

14.

So soon as there springs up within him an angry, malicious thought, some sinful, wrong disposition, ... he puts it away, removes it, destroys it, he makes it not to be. *Sabbâsava-sutta* (sec. 33).

15.

WITH not a thought of selfishness or covetous desire.

Fo-sho-hing-tsan-king (v. 167).

COVETOUSNESS and anger are as the serpent's poison.

Fo-sho-hing-tsan-king (v. 860).

16.

They who do evil go to hell; they who are righteous go to heaven.

Dhammapada (v. 126).

17.

He who, doing what he ought, ... gives pleasure to others, shall find joy in the other world.

Udânavarga (ch. 5, v. 26).

18.

And what is the purpose of every effort I make? It is that I may discharge the debt (which I owe) to other creatures, that I may make them happy in this world, and that they may gain heaven in the next.

Rock Inscriptions of Asoka (edict 6).

19.

He truly must have a loving heart,
For all things living place in him entire confidence.

Ta-chwang-yan-king-lun (sermon 62).

20.

OFTTIMES while he mused—as motionless
As the fixed rock his seat—the squirrel leaped
Upon his knee, the timid quail led forth
Her brood between his feet, and blue doves pecked
The rice-grains from the bowl beside his hand.

Sir Edwin Arnold (*Light of Asia*, bk. 5).

21.

FILLED with compassion for all creatures.

Saddharma-puṇḍarîka (ch. 13, v. 45).

WHO showeth mercy to every sentient being.

Udânavarga (ch. 31, v. 44).

22.

This (prince) feels for the welfare of the multitude.

Nâlaka-sutta (v. 15).

23.

The Royal Prince, perceiving the tired oxen, ... the men toiling beneath the midday sun, and the birds devouring the hapless insects, his heart was filled with grief, as a man would feel upon seeing his own household bound in fetters: thus was he touched with sorrow for the whole family of sentient creatures.

Fo-pen-hing-tsih-king (ch. 12).

24.

Because I love my realm, because my heart
Beats with each throb of all the hearts that ache.

Sir Edwin Arnold (*Light of Asia*, bk. 4).

25.

WHAT is a true gift?

One for which nothing is expected in return. *Prasnottaramâlikâ.*

26.

THERE is a way of giving, seeking pleasure by it, (or) coveting to get more; some also give to gain a name for charity, some to gain the happiness of heaven. ... But yours, O friend, is a charity free from such thoughts, the highest and best degree of charity, free from self-interest or thought of getting more.

Fo-sho-hing-tsan-king (vv. 1,517-9).

27.

'TIS thus men generally think and speak, they have a reference in all they do to their own advantage. But with this one it is not so: 'tis the good of others and not his own that he seeks.

Fo-pen-hing-tsih-king (ch. 20).

28.

Above all things be not careless; for carelessness is the great foe to virtue.

Fo-sho-hing-tsan-king (v. 2,081).

29.

You say that while young a man should be gay, and when old then religious. ... Death, however, as a robber, sword in hand, follows us all, desiring to capture his prey: how then should we wait for old age, ere we turn our minds to religion?

Fo-sho-hing-tsan-king (vv. 898-900).

30.

If you urge that I am young and tender, and that the time for seeking wisdom is not yet, then you should know that to seek true religion, there never is a time not fit.

Fo-sho-hing-tsan-king (vv. 439-40).

31

WORK out your own salvation with diligence.

Mahâparinibbâna-sutta (ch. 6).

No man can purify another.

Dhammapada (v. 165).

June.

I.

WHOSOEVER have incurred a fault, let him declare it.

Pâtimokkha (introduction).

2.

TRUST is the best of relationships.

Dhammapada (v. 204).

ABHOR dissimulation!

Fo-sho-hing-tsan-king (v. 2,023).

3.

FAITHFUL and trustworthy, he injures not his fellow man by deceit.

Tevijja-sutta (ch. 2).

4.

By the power of his compassion, ... he made all men friends.

Attanagalu-vansa (ch. 5, sec. 11).

5.

Since even animals can live together in mutual reverence, confidence, and courtesy, much more should you, O Brethren, so let your light shine forth that you ... may be seen to dwell in like manner together.

Cullavagga (khandhaka 6, ch. 6).

6.

Let us be knit together ... as friends.

Fo-sho-hing-tsan-king (v. 407).

Finding sweet comfort in united love.

Fo-sho-hing-tsan-king (v. 2,214).

7.

A PROUD heart leads to a vicious life.

Ta-chwang-yan-king-lun (sermon 45).

8.

LET him not therefore be proud, for that is not called bliss by the good.

Tuvaṭaka-sutta (v. 3).

UPRIGHT, conscientious, and of soft speech, gentle and not proud.

Metta-sutta (v. 1).

9.

TEACHING men to practise humility and lowliness.

Fo-sho-hing-tsan-king (v. 2,247).

10.

EVEN if a man have done evil a hundred times, let him not do it again.

Udânavarga (ch. 28, v. 21).

11.

HE who, having been angered, gives way to anger no more, has achieved a mighty victory.

Udânavarga (ch. 20, v. 17).

12.

BETTER than sovereignty over this earth, ... better than lordship over all worlds, is the recompense of the first step in holiness.

Dhammapada (v. 178).

13.

Now many distinguished warriors thought: We who go (to war) and find our delight in fighting, do evil. ... What shall we do that we may cease from evil and do good?

Mahâvagga (khandhaka 1, ch. 40).

14.

VICTORY breeds hatred.

Dhammapada (v. 201).

15.

THEREFORE has this pious inscription been carved (here on the rock), to the end that posterity may not suppose that any further conquest ought to be made by them. Let them not hold that conquest by the sword is worthy the name of conquest; let them see in it only confusion and violence. Let them reckon as true conquests none save the triumphs of religion.

Rock Inscriptions of Asoka (edict 13).

16.

He walks not in religion in a quarrelsome spirit.

Questions of King Milinda
(Book 4, ch. 1, sec. 9)

17.

Nay, friend, let not quarrel arise, nor strife, nor discord, nor dispute.

Mahâvagga (khandhaka 4, ch. 16).

18.

Thus he lives as a binder together of those who are divided, an encourager of those who are friends, a peace-maker, a lover of peace, impassioned for peace, a speaker of words that make for peace.

Tevijja-sutta (ch. 2).

19.

INDOLENCE is defilement.

Uṭṭhâna-sutta (v. 4).

BY work mankind exists.

Vâseṭṭha-sutta (v. 61).

20.

To give honour to those who are worthy of honour.

Mahâmaṅgala-sutta (v. 2).

21.

CAUSING destruction to living beings, killing and mutilating, ... stealing and speạking falsely, fraud and deception, ... these are (what defile a man).

Âmagandha-sutta (v. 4).

22.

Living in the world, and doing no harm to aught that lives.

Fo-pen-hing-tsih-king (ch. 39).

23.

Whether of the higher class of beings, as...a perfect man, a teacher,...or father,... or of the lower class of beings, as a grasshopper or the smallest insect—in one word, whatever hath life thou shalt not kill.

Sha-mi-lu-i-yao-lio.

24.

If a man thus walks in the ways of compassion, is it possible that he should hurt anything intentionally?

Sha-mi-lu-i-yao-lio.

25.

As he said so he acted.

Vaṅgîsa-sutta (v. 15).

26.

THOSE who have sin at heart, but are sweet of speech, are like a pitcher smeared with nectar, but full of poison.

Lalita Vistara (ch. 12).

LIKE a ... flower that is rich in colour, but has no scent, so are the fine ... words of him who does not act accordingly.

Dhammapada (v. 51).

27.

Now at that time men were speakers of truth, and keepers of their word when once they had pledged it.

Cullavagga (khandhaka 7, ch. 1).

28.

He whose mind is subdued and perfectly controlled is happy.

Udânavarga (ch. 31, v. 64).

29.

If only the thoughts be directed to that which is right, then happiness must necessarily follow.

Fa-kheu-pi-ü (sec. 11).

30.

This is the greatest happiness—to subdue the selfish thought of 'I.'

Udânavarga (ch. 30, v. 21).

July.

1.

Evil he overcame by righteousness.

Questions of King Milinda (Book 4, ch. 1, sec. 38).

He felt compassion towards those who tormented him.

Attanagalu-vansa (ch. 5, sec. 4).

2.

The bearer of ill-will towards them that bear ill-will can never become pure; but he who bears no ill-will pacifies them that hate.

Udânavarga (ch. 14, v. 12).

3.

The man who foolishly does me wrong, I will return him the protection of my ungrudging love: the more the evil that comes from him, the more the good that shall go from me.

Sûtra of Forty-two Sections (sec. 7).

4.

Even when much provocation is given, to be neither angry ... nor malicious.

Subha-sutta.

5.

To whom even the life of a serpent is sacred.

Lalita Vistara (ch. 1).

6.

I love living things that have no feet, ... four-footed creatures, and things with many feet. ... May all creatures, all things that live, all beings of whatever kind, may they all behold good fortune.

Cullavagga (khandhaka 5, ch. 6).

7.

Actions have their reward, and our deeds have their result.

Mahâvagga (khandhaka 1, ch. 38).

Our deeds are not lost, they will surely come (back again).

Kokâliya-sutta (v. 10).

8.

If thou art filled with the dread of suffering, if there is naught agreeable to thee in suffering, do no evil thing openly or even in secret.

Udânavarga (ch. 9, v. 3).

9.

Even could she have kept it secret from men, ... even could she have kept it secret from spirits, ... even could she have kept it secret from the gods, yet she could not have escaped herself from the knowledge of her sin.

Questions of King Milinda
(Book 4, ch. 4, sec. 43).

10.

Clad in garments pure as the moonbeams, ... her ornaments modesty and virtuous conduct.

Ajanta Cave Inscriptions.

11.

If you ... speak to a woman, do it with pureness of heart. ... Say to yourself: ... 'Placed in this sinful world, let me be as the spotless lily, unsoiled by the mire in which it grows.' Is she old? regard her as your mother. Is she honourable? as your sister. Is she of small account? as a younger sister. Is she a child? then treat her with reverence and politeness.

Sûtra of Forty-two Sections (sec. 28).

12.

Gentle and true, simple and kind was she,
Noble of mien, with gracious speech to all
And gladsome looks—a pearl of womanhood.

Sir Edwin Arnold (*Light of Asia*, bk. 6).

13.

Do not have evil-doers for friends. ... Take as your friends the best of men.

Dhammapada (v. 78).

14.

BRIEFLY I will tell you the marks of a friend—
When doing wrong, to warn; when doing well, to exhort to perseverance;
When in difficulty or danger, to assist, relieve, and deliver.
Such a man is indeed a true and illustrious friend.

Fo-pen-hing-tsih-king (ch. 16).

15.

HIS friendship is prized by the gentle and the good.

Fo-sho-hing-tsan-king (v. 1,506).

16.

LIVING ... without cruelty among the cruel.

Udânavarga (ch. 30, v. 47)

17.

THE Scripture saith: "Be kind and benevolent to every being, and spread peace in the world.... If it happen that thou see anything to be killed, thy soul shall be moved with pity and compassion. Ah, how watchful should we be over ourselves!"

Sha-mi-lu-i-yao-lio.

18.

I DESIRE to produce in myself a loving heart towards all living creatures.

Fo-pen-hing-tsih-king (ch. 7).

19.

LET us then practise good works, and inspect our thoughts that we do no evil.

Fo-sho-hing-tsan-king (vv. 1,642-3).

20.

Now, therefore, it behoves me to examine into my faults; and if I find anything wrong in me, to put it away, and practise virtue only.

Jâtaka 151.

21.

THEREFORE ... we would humble ourselves and repent us of our sins. Oh! that we may have strength to do so aright!

Liturgy of Kwan-yin.

22.

IF we know that we have done wrong, and yet refuse to acknowledge it, we are guilty of prevarication.

Chinese Pratimôksha.

23.

FROM the very first, ... having no wish to benefit others, or to do good in the least degree, ... we have been adding sin unto sin; and even though our actual crimes have not been so great, yet a wicked heart has ruled us within. Day and night, without interval or hesitation, have we continually contrived how to do wrong.

Liturgy of Kwan-yin.

24.

ACCEPT the confession I make of my sin in its sinfulness, to the end that in future I may restrain myself therefrom.

Cullavagga (khandhaka 5, ch. 20).

25.

He who offends an offenceless man, ... against such a fool the evil reverts, like fine dust thrown against the wind.

Kokâliya-sutta (v. 6).

26.

May wisdom be with me always.

Inscription in Temple of Nakhon Vat.

27.

The fool who knows his foolishness is wise at any rate so far. But the fool who thinks himself wise, he is a fool indeed.

Dhammapada (v. 63).

28.

He who holds back rising anger like a rolling chariot—him I call a real driver: other people are merely holding the reins.

Dhammapada (v. 222).

29.

Anger, alas! how it changes the comely face! how it destroys the loveliness of beauty!

Fo-sho-hing-tsan-king (v. 1,822).

30.

The fool who is angered and thinks to triumph by the use of abusive language, is always vanquished by him whose words are patient.

Udânavarga (ch. 20, v. 14).

31.

He who lives far from me yet walks righteously, is ever near me.

Fo-sho-hing-tsan-king (v. 1,980).

August.

I.

He sought after the good of those dependent on him.

Questions of King Milinda
(Book 4, ch. 4, sec. 43).

2.

Who, though he be lord over others, is patient with those that are weak.

Udânavarga (ch. 20, v. 8).

3.

Loving her maids and dependents even as herself.

Lalita Vistara (ch. 12).

4.

THE same measure as she applies to herself she applies likewise to other beings.

Saddharma-puṇḍarīka (ch. 11).

5.

LOVING all things which live even as themselves.

Sir Edwin Arnold (*Light of Asia*, bk. 8).

HEAR ye all this moral maxim, and having heard it keep it well: Whatsoever is displeasing to yourselves never do to another.

Bstan-hgyur (Mdo, vol. 123, leaf 174).

6.

THEN declared he unto them (the rule of doing to others what we ourselves like).

San-kiao-yuen-lieu.

7.

FROM henceforth ... put away evil and do good.

Jâtaka 6.

8.

AT morning, noon, and night successively, store up good works.

Fo-sho-hing-tsan-king (v. 2,039).

ALWAYS doing good to those around you.

Fo-pen-hing-tsih-king (ch. 38).

9.

IN order to terminate all suffering, be earnest in performing good deeds.

Buddhaghosa's Parables (ch. 8).

10.

Courteous and respectful to one another.

Jâtaka 37.

11.

Exhorting to virtue in the use of courteous language.

Fo-sho-hing-tsan-king (v. 171).

12.

Liberality, courtesy, benevolence, unselfishness, under all circumstances towards all people—these qualities are to the world what the linch-pin is to the rolling chariot.

Sigâlovâda-sutta.

13.

Persist not in calling attention to a matter calculated to cause division.

Pâtimokkha (Saṁghâdisesâ Dhammâ, sec. 10)

14.

Dwelling together in mutual love.

Brâhmaṇadhammika-sutta (v. 7).

15.

Let us now unite in the practice of what is good, cherishing a gentle and sympathizing heart, and carefully cultivating good faith and righteousness.

Travels of Fâ-hien (ch. 39).

16.

UNTAINTED, unselfish charity.

Fo-sho-hing-tsan-king (v. 1,501).

17.

FEELING deep compassion for the poor, grudging nothing which he possessed.

Phû-yau-king (kiouen 2).

18.

HUMBLE in mind, but large in gracious deeds, abundant in charity to the poor and helpless.

Fo-sho-hing-tsan-king (v. 1,438).

19.

FULL of modesty and pity, ... kind and compassionate to all creatures that have life.

Tevijja-sutta (ch. 2).

20.

HE who ... is tender to all that lives ... is protected by heaven and loved by men.

Fa-kheu-pi-ü (sec. 7).

21.

DAY and night the mind of Buddha's disciples always delights in compassion.

Dhammapada (v. 300).

22.

NOT praising himself for his virtues.

Duṭṭhaṭṭhaka-sutta (v. 4).

LET him not think detractingly of others.

Sâriputta-sutta (v. 19).

23.

BUT offer loving thoughts and acts to all.

Sir Edwin Arnold (*Light of Asia*, bk. 8).

24.

NEVER should he speak a disparaging word of anybody.

Saddharma-puṇḍarîka (ch. 13, v. 40).

LIGHTLY to laugh at and ridicule another is wrong.

Fa-kheu-pi-ü (sec. 17).

25.

WHATEVER I understand (to be right) ... I desire to practise.

Rock Inscriptions of Asoka
(Separate edicts, no. 1).

26.

VIRTUOUS deeds should be practised to-day; for who can say but we may die to-morrow?

Temee Jatu.

SHORT indeed is the life of man; within a hundred years he dies; or if any one lives longer, then he dies of old age.

Jarâ-sutta (v. 1).

27.

MAY I be thoroughly imbued with benevolence, and show alway a charitable disposition, till such time as this heart shall cease to beat.

Inscription in Temple of Nakhon Vat.

28.

Born to give joy and bring peace to the world.

Fo-pen-hing-tsih-king (ch. 9).

The whole world of sentient creatures enjoyed ... universal tranquility.

Fo-sho-hing-tsan-king (v. 34).

29.

Enmity and envy gave way to peace; contentment and rest prevailed everywhere; ... discord and variance were entirely appeased.

Fo-sho-hing-tsan-king (v. 133).

30.

Creatures of every variety were moved one toward another lovingly; fear and terror altogether put away, none entertained a hateful thought; ... the Devas, foregoing their heavenly joys, sought rather to alleviate the sinner's sufferings.

Fo-sho-hing-tsan-king (vv. 1,172-3).

31.

LOVING virtue, he is able to profit men; and thus, by an impartiality of conduct, he treats them all ... as his own equals and fellows.

Fa-kheu-pi-ū (sec. 38).

September.

I.

VICE, O king, is a mean thing, virtue is great and grand.

Questions of King Milinda (Book 4, ch. 8, sec. 31).

2.

LET him do nothing mean.

Metta-sutta (v. 3).

I DEEM ... unrighteous actions contemptible.

Mahâvagga (khandhaka 6, ch. 31).

3.

HE sustains his life by means that are quite pure.

Tevijja-sutta (ch. 1).

4.

Men going (to what they deserve) according to their deeds.

Salla-sutta (v. 14).

5.

As men sow, thus shall they reap.

Ta-chwang-yan-king-lun (sermon 57).

6.

Reaping the fruit of right or evil doing, and sharing happiness or misery in consequence.

Fo-sho-hing-tsan-king (v. 1,118).

7.

YOUR evil thoughts and evil words but hurt yourselves.

Fo-sho-hing-tsan-king (v. 2,047).

PEOPLE grieve from selfishness.

Jarâ-sutta (v. 2).

8.

THE evil-doer suffers both in this world and in the next.

Dhammapada (v. 17).

9.

HELL was not created by any one. ... The fire of the angry mind produces the fire of hell, and consumes its possessor. When a person does evil, he lights the fire of hell, and burns with his own fire.

Mulamuli.

10.

Doing good we reap good, just as a man who sows that which is sweet (enjoys the same).

Fa-kheu-pi-ü (sec. 20).

11.

He who does wrong, O king, comes to feel remorse. ... But he who does well feels no remorse, and feeling no remorse, gladness will spring up within him.

Questions of King Milinda
(Book 3, ch. 7, sec. 7).

12.

Morality brings happiness: ... at night one's rest is peaceful, and on waking one is still happy.

Udânavarga (ch. 6, v. 3).

13.

IF, then, you would please me, show pity to that poor wretch. *Nâgânanda* (act 3).

OPPRESSED with others' suffering.

Fo-sho-hing-tsan-king (v. 338).

14.

A LOVING heart is the great requirement! to regard the people as an only son; not to oppress, not to destroy; ... not to exalt oneself by treading down others, but to comfort and befriend those in suffering.

Fo-sho-hing-tsan-king (vv. 1632-4).

15.

HE cares for and cherishes his people more than one would a naked and perishing child. *Fo-pen-hing-tsih-king* (ch. 8).

To give help to the impoverished, the orphan, and the aged.

Fa-kheu-pi-ü (sec. 18).

16.

THE acts and the practice of religion, to wit, sympathy, charity, truthfulness, purity, gentleness, kindness.

Pillar Inscriptions of Asoka (edict 8).

17.

Go ye, O Brethren, and wander forth, for the gain of the many, the welfare of the many, in compassion for the world, for the good, for the gain, for the welfare of ... men. ... Publish, O Brethren, the doctrine glorious. ... Preach ye a life of holiness ... perfect and pure.

Mahávagga (khandhaka 1, ch. 11).

18.

Go, then, through every country, convert those not converted. ... Go! therefore, each one travelling alone; filled with compassion, go! rescue and receive.

Fo-sho-hing-tsan-king (vv. 1,299 and 1,300).

19.

HAVE you not heard what Buddha says in the Sûtra, (where he bids his followers) not to despise the little child?

Ta-chwang-yan-king-lun (sermon 3).

20.

In this mode of salvation there are no distinctions of rich and poor, male and female, people and priests: all are equally able to arrive at the blissful state.

From a Chinese Buddhist Tract.

21.

EVEN the most unworthy who seeks for salvation is not to be forbidden.

Ta-chwang-yan-king-lun (sermon 55).

LOOK with friendship ... on the evil and on the good.

Introduction to Jâtaka Book (v. 169).

22.

SHOULD those who are not witn us, O Brethren, speak in dispraise of me,* or of my doctrine, or of the church, that is no reason why you should give way to anger.

Brahma-jâla-sutta.

23.

WHY should there be such sorrowful contention? You honour what we honour, both alike: then we are brothers as concerns religion.

Fo-sho-hing-tsan-king (vv. 2,264-5).

24.

No decrying of other sects, ... no depreciation (of others) without cause, but on the contrary, a rendering of honour to other sects for whatever cause honour is due. By so doing, both one's own sect will be helped forward, and other sects benefited; by acting otherwise, one's own sect will be destroyed in injuring others.

Rock Inscriptions of Asoka (edict 12)

* Buddha.

25.

But if others walk not righteously, we ought by righteous dealing to appease them: in this way, by showing its advantage, we cause religion everywhere to take deep hold and abide.

Fo-sho-hing-tsan-king (v. 2,274).

26.

Who is a (true) spiritual teacher?

He who, having grasped the essence of things, ever seeks to be of use to other beings.

Prasnottaramâlikâ.

27.

Tell him ... I look for no recompense—not even to be born in heaven—but seek ... the benefit of men, to bring back those who have gone astray, to enlighten those living in ... dismal error, ... to put away all sources of sorrow and pain from the world.

Fo-pen-hing-tsih-king (ch. 18).

28.

I CONSIDER the welfare of all people as something for which I must work.

Rock Inscriptions of Asoka (edict 6).

29.

THEN the man ... said to himself: "I will not keep all this treasure to myself; I will share it with others." Upon this he went to king Brahmadatta, and said: ... "Be it known to you I have discovered a treasure, and I wish it to be used for the good of the country."

Fo-pen-hing-tsih-king (ch. 60)

30.

FOR the benefit, weal, and happiness of the people generally.

Saddharma-puṇḍarîka (ch. 7).

October.

1.

WITH no selfish or partial joy ... they rejoiced.

Fo-sho-hing-tsan-king (v. 24).

2.

IF thou see others lamenting, join in their lamentations: if thou hear others rejoicing, join in their joy.

Jitsu-go-kiyô.

3.

MY son, tell me thy sorrow, that it may become more endurable by participation.

Nâgânanda (act 5).

4.

LET the wise man guard his thoughts, for they are ... very artful and rush whereso-ever they list.

Dhammapada (v. 36).

5.

To think no evil and do none: on the contrary, to benefit all creatures.

Fo-pen-hing-tsih-king (ch. 15).

6.

EVERY variety of living creature I must ever defend from harm.

Ta-chwang-yan-king-lun (sermon 62).

7.

WHEN thou seest righteousness, quickly follow it: when thou seest iniquity, instantly flee.

Jitsu-go-kiyô.

8.

DISGUSTED ... with all sins.

Sabhiya-sutta (v. 22).

9.

MAY I never, even in a dream, be guilty of theft, adultery, drunkenness, life-slaughter, and untruthfulness.

Attanagalu-vansa (conclusion).

10.

Spotless even as the moon, pure, serene, and undisturbed.

Vâseṭṭha-sutta (v. 44).

11.

Practise the most perfect virtue.

Udânavarga (ch. 28, v. 1).

To attain perfection that he may profit others.

Fo-pen-hing-tsih-king (ch. 24).

12.

The present is an imperfect existence: ... I pray for greater perfection in the next.

Inscription in Temple of Nakhon Vat.

13.

FULFIL the perfection of long-suffering; be thou paṭient under ... reproach.

Introduction to Jâtaka Book.

14.

MY duty is to bear all the insults which the heretics launch against me.

Buddhaghosa's Parables (ch. 5).

15.

SILENTLY shall I endure abuse, as the elephant in battle endures the arrow sent from the bow.

Dhammapada (v. 320).

16.

Let not the member of Buddha's order tremble at blame, neither let him puff himself up when praised.

Tuvaṭaka-sutta (v. 14).

Cultivate equanimity.

Nâlaka-sutta (v. 24).

17.

There are two extremes ... which he who has given up the world should avoid— ... a life devoted to pleasures: ... this is degrading, sensual, ... ignoble; ... and a life given to mortifications: this is painful ... and profitless.

Mahâvagga (khandhaka 1, ch. 6).

18.

The end of the pleasures of sense is as the lightning flash: ... what profit, then, in doing iniquity?

Fo-sho-hing-tsan-king (v. 1,645).

19.

He speaks truth unmixed with falsehood.

Sâmañña-phala-sutta.

There is (guilt calling for repentance) in prevarication.

Pâtimokkha (Pâcittiyâ Dhammâ, sec. 12).

20.

He that praises him who should be blamed, or blames him who should be praised, gathers up sin thereby in his mouth.

Kokâliya-sutta (v. 2).

21.

In four ways may the flatterer be known a false friend—he assents when you do wrong; he assents when you do right; he sounds your praises before your face, and speaks ill of you behind your back.

Sigâlovâda-sutta.

22.

THE member of Buddha's order ... should abstain ... from theft, even of a blade of grass.

Mahâvagga (khandhaka I, ch. 78).

23.

FROM bribery, cheating, fraud, and (all other) crooked ways he abstains.

Tevijja-sutta (ch. 2).

24.

THE Scripture moveth us, therefore, rather to cut off the hand than to take anything which is not ours.

Sha-mi-lu-i-yao-lio.

25.

ALL the people were bound close in family love and friendship.

Fo-sho-hing-tsan-king v. 139).

26.

I GIVE up my own will, and live only according to the will of these ... brethren.

Mahâvagga (khandhaka 10, ch. 4).

27.

THENCEFORTH he devoted himself to caring for others alone.

Questions of King Milinda (Book 4, ch. 1, sec. 37).

28.

EVEN as the lily lives upon and loves the water,
So Upatissa and Kolita likewise,
Joined by closest bond of love,
If by necessity compelled to live apart,
Were overcome by grief and aching heart.
Fo-pen-hing-tsih-king (ch. 47).

29.

(THE true friend) forsakes you not in trouble; he will lay down his life for your sake. *Sigâlovâda-sutta.*

30.

IN grief as well as in joy we are united,
In sorrow and in happiness alike.
* * * *
That which your heart rejoices in as good,
That I also rejoice in and follow.
It were better I should die with you,
Than ... attempt to live where you are not.
Fo-pen-hing-tsih-king (ch. 48).

31.

LET not the member of Buddha's order be a boaster.

Tuvaṭaka-sutta (v. 16).

GLORY not in thyself, but rather in thy neighbour.

Siamese Buddhist Maxim.

November.

1.

THOSE who have no faults of their own may reprove others; but if a man guilty of the same crime reproves another for it, he ... excites laughter against himself.

Ta-chwang-yan-king-lun (sermon 19).

2.

JUDGE not thy neighbour.

Siamese Buddhist Maxim.

FAULT is not to be found unnecessarily.

Ta-chwang-yan-king-lun (sermon 17).

3.

WHAT is it to you ... whether another is guilty or guiltless? Come, friend, atone for your own offence.

Mahâvagga (khandhaka 2, ch. 27).

NOT doing what he has himself blamed.

Guhaṭṭhaka-sutta (v. 7).

4.

EVEN a king may be full of trouble; but a common man, who is holy, has rest everlasting.

Fo-sho-hing-tsan-king (v. 1,623).

5.

YE, then, my followers, ... give not way ... to sorrow; ... aim to reach the home where separation cannot come.

Fo-sho-hing-tsan-king (vv. 2,097-8).

NIRVÂṆA, ... the source of the beauty of holiness, ... Nirvâṇa, beautiful in righteousness.

Questions of King Milinda
(Book 4, ch. 8, secs. 70 and 74).

6.

THIS world is afflicted with death and decay; therefore the wise do not grieve, knowing the terms of the world.

Salla-sutta (v. 8).

7.

LOVING and merciful towards all.

Fo-sho-hing-tsan-king (v. 1,091).

FILLED with universal benevolence.

Fa-kheu-pi-ū (sec. 27).

8.

A FRIEND to all creatures in the world.

Saddharma-puṇḍarika (ch. 13, v. 59).

9.

BENT on promoting the happiness of a created beings.

Lalita Vistara (ch. 7)

10.

CONQUER thy greediness for sensual pleasures.

Jatukaṇṇimâṇavapucchâ (v. 3).

THEREFORE should we encourage small desire, that we may have to give to him who needs.

Fo-sho-hing-tsan-king (v. 2,058).

11.

JUSTLY I seek for riches, and having sought for riches justly, I give of my ... justly acquired wealth to one, to two, to three, ... to a hundred.

Mâgha-sutta (preamble).

12.

THEY sought their daily gain righteously; no covetous, money-loving spirit prevailed; with pious intent they gave liberally; there was not a thought of any reward.

Fo-sho-hing-tsan-king (vv. 140-1).

13.

THERE is in charity a proper time and a proper mode.

Fo-sho-hing-tsan-king (v. 1,505).

14.

BETTER would it be to swallow a red-hot iron ball, than that a bad, unrestrained fellow should live on the charity of the land.

Dhammapada (v. 308).

15.

OUR duty to do something, not only for our own benefit, but for the good of those who shall come after us.

Fo-pen-hing-tsih-king (ch. 43).

16.

HAVE respect for the aged as though they were thy father and mother: love the young as thy children or younger brethren.

Jitsu-go-kiyô.

17.

TAKE me, then, quickly hence and go, and going, never more come back with me! For since you have not brought back (my noble son), my life is no more worth preserving!

Fo-sho-hing-tsan-king (v. 648).

18.

HAPPY ... is the man that honours his father: he also that honours his mother is happy.

Udânavarga (ch. 30, v. 23).

19.

THIS good man, moved by pity, gives up his life for another, as though it were but a straw.

Nâgânanda (act 4).

20.

THE man of wisdom should do what is beneficial to other beings, by abstaining from selfish aspirations even so far as to sacrifice his own body.

Kathâ Sarit Sâgara (ch. 28).

21.

HE is my husband. I love and revere him with all my heart, and therefore am determined to share his fate. Kill me first, ... and afterwards do to him as you list.

Fo-pen-hing-tsih-king (ch. 51).

22.

WHAT has been designated 'name' and 'family' ... is but a term.

Vâseṭṭha-sutta (v. 55).

REVERENCE ... is due to righteous conduct.

Fo-sho-hing-tsan-king (v. 532).

23.

THE wise man ... regards with reverence all who deserve reverence, without distinction of person.

Ta-chwang-yan-king-lun (sermon 16).

24.

FOR if virtue flags and folly rules, what reverence can there be ... for a high name or boast of prowess, inherited from former generations?

Fo-sho-hing-tsan-king (v. 830).

25.

Whosoever exalts himself and despises others, becoming mean by his pride, let us know such as a 'base-born.'

Vasala-sutta (v. 17).

26.

In every condition, high or low, we find folly and ignorance, (and men) carelessly following the dictates of ... passion.

Fo-sho-hing-tsan-king (v. 716).

27.

Whosoever strikes, or by words annoys, mother or father, brother or sister, ... let us know such as a 'base-born.'

Vasala-sutta (v. 10).

28.

Fools of little understanding have themselves for their greatest enemies, for they do evil deeds which cannot but bear bitter fruit.

Dhammapada (v. 66).

29.

There is not a spot upon earth, neither in the sky, neither in the sea, neither ... in the mountain-clefts, where an (evil) deed does not bring trouble (to the doer).

Udânavarga (ch. 9, v. 5).

30.

Surely if living creatures saw the consequence of all their evil deeds, ... with hatred would they turn and leave them, fearing the ruin following.

Fo-sho-hing-tsan-king (vv. 1,124-5).

December.

I.

For all men), as for (my) children, I desire ... complete happiness and welfare.

Rock Inscriptions of Asoka
(Separate edicts, no. 1).

2.

He lets his mind pervade one quarter of the world with thoughts of love, and so the second, and so the third, and so the fourth. And thus the whole wide world, above, below, around, and everywhere, he continues to pervade with heart of love, far-reaching, grown great, and beyond measure.

Tevijja-sutta (ch. 3).

3.

Whatsoever living beings there are, feeble or strong, ... small or large, seen or not seen, ... may all creatures be happy-minded.

Metta-sutta (vv. 4-5).

4.

A WISE man never resents with passion the abuse of the foolish.

Ta-chwang-yan-king-lun (sermon 27).

5.

YIELD not (one moment) to the angry impulse.

Fo-sho-hing-tsan-king (v. 1,824).

OVERCOME anger by love.

Dhammapada (v. 223).

6.

LIKE as the lotus ... is untarnished by the water, so is Nirvâṇa by any evil dispositions.

Questions of King Milinda
(Book 4, ch. 8, sec. 66).

7.

In agreement with all men, and hurting nobody, ... he, as far as possible, does good to all. *Fo-pen-hing-tsih-king* (ch. 15).

8.

Reverently practising the four gracious acts—
Benevolence, charity, humanity, love;
Doing all for the good of men, and that they in turn may benefit others.
Phû-yau-king (kiouen 2).

9.

They also,* resigning the deathless bliss within their reach,
Worked the welfare of mankind in various lands.
What man is there who would be remiss in doing good to mankind?
(*Quoted by Max Müller*, "Selected Essays," vol. 2).

* Buddhist missionaries.

10.

When first I undertook to obtain wisdom,
Then also I took on me to defend (the weak).
All living things of whatsoever sort
Call forth my compassion and pity.

Ta-chwang-yan-king-lun (sermon 62).

11.

After having refrained from hurting all beings, both those that are strong and those that tremble in the world.

Dhammika-sutta (v. 19).

12.

Because the dove fears the hawk,
With fluttering pennons she comes to seek my protection.
Though she cannot speak with her mouth,
Yet through fear her eyes are moist.
Now, therefore, I will extend (to this poor creature)
My own protection and defence.

Ta-chwang-yan-king-lun (sermon 62).

13.

An unselfish virtuous man.

Muni-sutta (v. 14).

The outward form not affecting religion.

Fo-sho-hing-tsan-king (v. 1,290).

14.

Neither is it right to judge men's character by outward appearances.

Ta-chwang-yan-king-lun (sermon 3).

15.

The body may wear the ascetic's garb, the heart be immersed in worldly thoughts: ... the body may wear a worldly guise, the heart mount high to things celestial.

Fo-sho-hing-tsan-king (vv. 1,290-1).

16.

FULL of truth and compassion and mercy and long-suffering.

Jâtaka 35.

17.

UPRIGHTNESS is his delight.

Tevijja-sutta (ch. 1).

18.

MAKING ... virtue always his first aim.

Fa-kheu-pi-ü (sec. 39).

AN example for all the earth.

Fo-sho-hing-tsan-king (v. 173).

19.

WHAT he hears here he repeats not there, to raise a quarrel against the people here. *Tevijja-sutta* (ch. 2).

HE injures none by his conversation. *Sâmañña-phala-sutta.*

20.

AIMING to curb the tongue, ... aiming to benefit the world.

Fo-sho-hing-tsan-king (vv. 168-9).

21.

INTENT upon benefiting thy fellow-creatures. *Kathâ Sarit Sâgara* (ch. 72).

WALK in the path of duty, do good to your brethren, and work no evil towards them. *Avadâna Sataka* (story 38).

22.

HEALTH is the greatest of gifts, contentment the best of riches.

Dhammabada (v. 204).

23.

IF thou be born in the poor man's hovel, yet have wisdom, then wilt thou be like the lotus-flower growing out of the mire.

Jitsu-go-kivô.

24.

THE rich who is not contented endures the pain of poverty.

Fo-sho-hing-tsan-king (v 2,062).

25.

THE words of Buddha, even when stern, yet ... as full of pity as the words of a father to his children.

Questions of King Milinda
(Book 4, ch. 3, sec. 18).

26.

OVERCOMING all enemies by the force (of his love).

Fo-sho-hing-tsan-king (v. 2,148).

27.

How great his pity and his love toward those who opposed his claims, neither rejoicing in their defeat, nor yet exulting in his own success!

Fo-sho-hing-tsan-king (v. 2,144).

28.

The Buddha has mercy even on the meanest thing.

Cullavagga (khandhaka 5, ch. 21).

29.

He that ... would wait upon me,* let him wait on the sick.

Mahâvagga (khandhaka 8, ch. 26).

The Buddha, O king, magnifies not the offering ot gifts to himself, but rather to whomsoever ... is deserving.

Questions of King Milinda (Book 4, ch. 6, sec. 14).

30.

If you desire to honour Buddha, follow the example of his patience and long-suffering.

Fo-sho-hing-tsan-king (v. 2,242).

* Buddha.

31.

RADIANT with heavenly pity, lost in care
For those he knew not, save as fellow-lives.

Sir Edwin Arnold (*Light of Asia*, bk. 5).

WHO that hears of him, but yearns with love?

Fo-sho-hing-tsan-king (v. 2,305).